WHAT'S NEXT? WHAT'S NEXT?

?

THE FUTURE OF

Architecture

By Lori Dittmer

CREATIVE EDUCATION

TABLE OF
Contents

Introduction…4

A History of Building…6

Architecture Becomes a Profession…13

Motivations for Improvement…14

Consumerism or Conservation?…16

Green Methods Unproven…22

Elevators Lift People, Buildings…25

Designs on the Future…28

Preservation Versus Conservation…30

Merging Homes with Nature…33

Creativity and Collaboration…36

H. G. Wells Predicts Arcology…39

World's Fair Stretches Imaginations…40

Glossary…44

Selected Bibliography…46

Web Sites…46

Index…47

INTRODUCTION

What if, instead of shingles and siding, your house was covered with a substance similar to lizard skin, which could change its color depending on the weather and heal itself from damage caused by exposure to sun, wind, and hail? On sunny days, the "skin" would turn dark and keep excess heat away from the house. On cloudy days, it would become clear to let in as much heat and light as possible. This same skin would collect rainwater and **condensation** to use for taking showers, washing dishes, and doing laundry.

Scientists are working on making these features possible. In fact, "self-healing" paints already exist and are used in the paint on some cars. When the surface of the paint is scratched, tiny capsules break open to release more color. Developing and adapting these ideas for use in buildings, though, will take time and money, which many people aren't willing to pay just yet. Many architects agree that the future of building will focus on ways to reduce pollution, conserve energy, and save space on the planet for the world's ever growing population. Some of this new architecture will come from futuristic designs, upgrades on current technology, and new materials inspired by plants and animals, such as weather-sensitive skin on a house. At the same time, architects are today finding inspiration in the past, peering back into history to study how ancient builders constructed energy-efficient homes suited to their location.

Architecture's future
may include structural
designs that leave
traditional wood
and paint far behind
in favor of flexible
surfaces that resemble
reptilian scales

A HISTORY OF BUILDING

Humankind has been building structures for thousands of years. Architecture—the science and art of building—began among prehistoric farming communities, when people settled in one place for long periods of time. Looking at the remains of ancient structures, scientists have been able to determine how societies lived and what they believed was important at the time. Temples were among the first products of architecture. Often, temples were built as a way to reach toward heaven and were aligned with the sun and patterns in the stars. The earliest temples—such as the Ziggurat of Ur in Sumer, which is now southern Iraq—were shaped from sun-dried clay bricks into stepped pyramids called ziggurats.

The early Egyptians left behind several architectural **remnants** of their lives. The pyramids were built as tombs for deceased pharaohs, or kings, as well as their valuable earthly possessions, which the people believed they could use again after they died. A pyramid was developed with secret underground passageways and rooms, as well as traps to keep out grave robbers, and it was an impressive monument to the deceased. Roughly 4,700 years ago, Imhotep, possibly the earliest known architect, designed the Step Pyramid of Djoser (or Zoser) at Saqqara. To build this 204-foot-tall (62 m) pyramid, laborers rafted huge granite blocks up the Nile River and dragged them on wooden rollers to the proper location. These huge blocks, possibly 2.5 tons (2.3 t) each, were pushed up mud ramps and levered into place.

The pyramids (left) and ziggurats (below) of the ancient world were massive structures, as achieving great height required huge bases under the tapered peaks

The most famous Egyptian buildings are the three Pyramids of Giza, clustered together near the city of Cairo. Together, these pyramids represent one of the seven wonders of the ancient world, and the largest, the pyramid of Khufu, is one of the biggest buildings ever. Made from 2.3 million blocks of limestone, the pyramid is 481 feet (147 m) high. Experts estimate that as many as 100,000 men worked for 30 years to finish the structure.

The ancient Greeks learned from the Egyptians, creating **columns** and using precise mathematical concepts to build their temples in a way that would be pleasing to the eye. Their open-air temples were built in honor of Greek gods such as Zeus and Poseidon. The greatest example is the Parthenon, which was rebuilt after the Persian Empire invaded Athens in 480 B.C. and destroyed the original structure. Designed by the Greek architects Ictinus and Callicrates, the Parthenon, which means "place of the maiden," honors Athena Parthenos, goddess of war and wisdom. The temple was built to represent the ideas important to Greek culture. The columns symbolize the loom, commonly used in Greek homes for weaving. The columns surround the structure as the people gathered around Athena, whose statue stood at the center of the building. The columns are not completely straight but bulge slightly. Historians once believed this to be an imperfection in the structure, but researchers now believe that the columns were meant to lean and curve ever so slightly. Vitruvius, a Roman engineer and architect

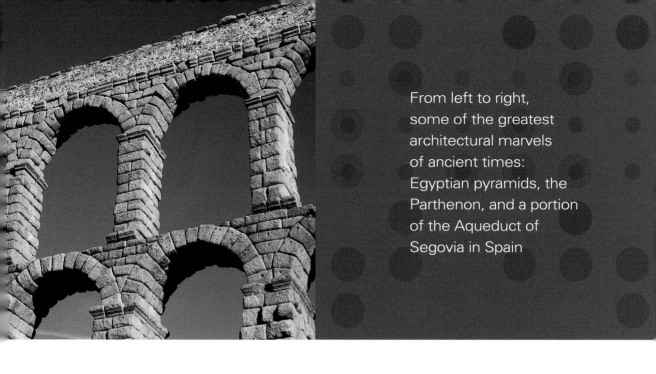

From left to right, some of the greatest architectural marvels of ancient times: Egyptian pyramids, the Parthenon, and a portion of the Aqueduct of Segovia in Spain

of the early first century B.C., wrote that Greek architecture used a method called *alexemata*, or "betterments," to improve the look of the columns. The temple's base curves slightly upward toward the center, while the columns lean slightly inward.

When the Romans took over Greece and much of what is now Europe by around 100 B.C., they embraced Greek architecture and worked to improve it. The Romans introduced personal comforts such as baths, sewers, and underfloor heating. They masterfully employed arches to create **aqueducts** that brought water into the city. During the reign of the emperor Augustus (27 B.C.–A.D. 14), the Romans began using sheets of marble for walls, held together by an invention called cement. Although the cement that builders use today is made from chalk and clay, the Romans mixed ground volcanic ash with water. A chemical reaction transformed the mix into an artificial stone. The Roman Empire reached into three continents, enabling rulers to gather a variety of beautiful marble stones, including yellow from Tunisia, purple from Turkey, and green-black from Greece. All these types of marble were used in the creation of the Pantheon, completed in Rome in A.D. 126 as a rebuilt temple to all Roman gods. The temple was topped by a 142-foot-wide (43 m) dome—the widest in the world until the 19th century. This dome, designed by the emperor and architect Hadrian, was made with layers of concrete on a temporary wooden frame and features a central opening to the sky.

The Great Wall of
China (below) and
castles such as the
Tower of London
(opposite) were
created largely with
defense in mind, with
tall and thick walls

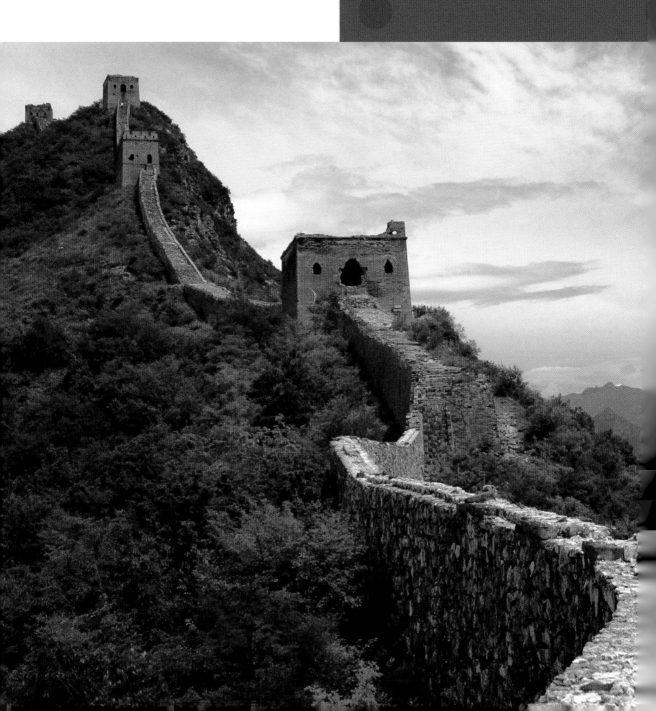

While the Roman Empire was still in its prime and spreading buildings and roads across Europe, the Chinese were constructing another masterpiece: the Great Wall. Largely completed in about 206 B.C. during the reign of the first emperor of China, Qin Shi Huang, the wall extended about 4,500 miles (7,245 km) along the northern boundary of the empire. Laborers used the materials readily available, such as earth, sand, stones, and reeds, to build the wall, which varied in height from 26 to 46 feet (7.9–14 m).

An old English proverb states that "a man's home is his castle," an idea that likely stemmed from the Middle Ages, roughly A.D. 476 to 1453. This time period is known for its towering castles, such as England's Tower of London, started in the 1070s by William the Conqueror. Places of worship also became the focal points of great architecture. The Roman emperor Justinian employed the architects Anthemius of Tralles and Isidore of Miletus to design the Hagia Sophia, also known as the Church of the Holy Wisdom, in Constantinople in 532. The structure reached completion after only five years, which was a major accomplishment. Topped with a wide but shallow dome encircled by 40 windows, the Hagia Sophia's system of vaults and further use of windows allowed sunlight to flood its interior. Such a style was a breakthrough in architecture.

By the mid-1800s, builders were turning to a new material: cast iron. It was cheaper and stronger than stone, and pieces of it could be **prefabricated** and shipped to the building site. Many architects

used iron as supports that were hidden beneath stone, brick, and other materials thought to be more attractive. That's why French engineer Alexandre Gustave Eiffel caused controversy with his iron-clad Eiffel Tower, completed in Paris in 1889. At 984 feet (300 m) in height, it was the tallest building in the world, and each of its approximately 18,000 iron pieces was made in Eiffel's factory rather than onsite. Despite numerous critics who called the structure useless, too tall, and even "monstrous," the tower remained and is now one of the most visited and **iconic** structures in the world. "There is an attractive element in the colossal," Eiffel noted.

ARCHITECTURE BECOMES A PROFESSION

Historians regard Andrea Palladio, born in 1508 in Italy, as the first modern architect. Unlike those before him, Palladio committed himself fully to his work as an architect rather than also working as a sculptor, painter, or craftsman. Palladio brought elements from Classical style into his designs. One of his most famous and often imitated buildings was the Villa Capra in Vicenza, Italy, which featured a **portico** *on each side and a dome inspired by the Pantheon. Palladio created the Villa Capra as a retreat for the wealthy to escape the city, and the design was the inspiration for American president Thomas Jefferson's home in Monticello, Virginia, nearly 200 years later.*

The Eiffel Tower's distinctive and groundbreaking use of uncovered iron made the structure very strong, as winds could blow through it with little resistance

The 20th century witnessed a flurry of building activity in the United States. By then, English inventor Sir Henry Bessemer had developed the **Bessemer process**, which allowed workers to more quickly and cheaply convert iron to steel, a lighter yet stronger metal. In the late 1920s, architects William Van Alen and H. Craig Severance engaged one another in a heated race to build the tallest skyscraper in New York. Severance's tower, the 927-foot (283 m) 40 Wall Street, reached completion first in Manhattan. Van Alen, who had discovered Severance was planning to beat him by 2 feet (61 cm), then produced a secret, 125-foot (38 m) steel spire for the top of his skyscraper, called the Chrysler Building. His bragging rights didn't last long, though. Within two years, the Empire State Building towered above both skyscrapers. At 1,250 feet (381 m), it would remain the world's tallest building until 1972. Critics compared these towering skyscrapers to glass and metal filing cabinets, but the quest to "go bigger" would continue.

MOTIVATIONS FOR IMPROVEMENT

Architects are continuously working to improve their designs. Some may do so for selfish reasons, while others are more concerned with helping others, including future generations. Many architects who have designed skyscrapers have sought the fame of creating the tallest building in the world. For decades, taller and taller skyscrapers have topped each other to become famous for their height, regardless of what's inside them. Architects have also been changing their designs to use solar and wind energy, saving natural resources and the planet's environment. Other architects have their eyes on protecting people in the event of worldwide **catastrophes**.

New York City's Chrysler Building is notable for its Art Deco style; the Art Deco movement peaked in the 1920s and was known for its ornamental curves

CHAPTER TWO

2

CONSUMERISM OR CONSERVATION?

In recent years, the world has witnessed the rise of new, **opulent** towers and other architectural marvels, particularly in Asia. In preparation for the 2008 Summer Olympics in Beijing, the Chinese government employed more than a million workers to build several structures. The National Stadium, resembling a steel bird's nest, was the focal point of the Games. The National Grand Theater was constructed to look like a huge, **titanium** egg, and the aquatics center appeared to be covered in soap bubbles that glowed blue at night. The "bubbles" were made with a new material called ethylene tetrafluoroethylene (ETFE)—a type of plastic that is only one percent the weight of glass and much cheaper to install. DuPont, an American chemical company, originally developed the

The Olympic Games
have generated
magnificent buildings,
including Beijing's
National Stadium
(opposite), National
Grand Theater (above),
and Water Cube (right)

The Burj Al Arab (its helipad visible at top left) is truly one of the most distinctive buildings in the world; some of the hotel's rooms cost $27,000 per night

material to be used as insulation for the **aeronautics** industry, but because it is strong and resists corrosion, ETFE's potential for use in construction appears promising.

Dubai, one of seven emirates, or political territories, comprising the United Arab Emirates (UAE), has also experienced an explosion of cutting-edge building and design. Completed in 1999, the Burj Al Arab, one of the world's tallest hotels, stands on 250 concrete piles that go down into the seafloor. Resembling an Arab sailing ship with the sail billowing out, the hotel has a **Teflon** coating to help control the temperature inside. Meant to appeal to the super-rich, the Burj Al Arab has a helipad on top for guests' private aircraft to land. Even the island it sits on was man-made.

Dubai's latest achievement, the Burj Khalifa, which opened in 2010, became the tallest building on Earth upon its completion. At 2,717 feet (828 m), the Burj—which means "tower" and is named for the president of the UAE, Sheikh Khalifa bin Zayed Al Nahyan—dwarfs all other competitors. If the Empire State Building could be stacked on top of the Chrysler Building, the resulting structure still wouldn't equal the Burj Khalifa. The bottom of the building is shaped like a "Y" laid flat, and the lowest 20 stories are large to give the tower a wide base. As it rises, the structure narrows, which gives the tower a slender, appealing shape that stands in contrast to the boxlike appearance of many skyscrapers. In fact, the tower has a different shape at each level, which protects it from the stress of strong winds. Most of the space within the Burj has been devoted to condominium apartments. Investors hope that rich business people and tourists purchase the units for temporary visits. After all, in addition to having a view from the top of the built world, visitors do not have far to go to reach one of the world's largest shopping centers, as well as one of the world's only indoor ski slopes, both of which are in Dubai.

But while one movement in architecture today involves building to excess and drawing tourism, another is leaning toward "green" building—using fewer **fossil fuels** and putting less pollution into the environment. Although recycling, turning off lights, and finding new ways to heat and cool homes are measures of conserving energy, there is a growing awareness that the energy required to turn clay into bricks, melt and process steel, and transport these materials to factories is astounding. For example, roughly 400 trees are burned to produce 25,000 bricks.

Green building has made architects step back from the International Style that has been at the forefront of architecture for decades. International Style allows India to build the same structure as the U.S. Any country in nearly any climate can produce a steel-and-glass skyscraper with artificial heating, cooling, and lighting. In green building (also known as sustainable building), architects consider the climate and location of the building site and create a structure specifically for that area. A site that receives many hours of sunshine but is largely shielded from wind would do well with solar panels but not wind turbines, for instance. Surprisingly, the

The almost impossibly tall Burj Khalifa, built at a cost of $1.5 billion, was the product of international collaboration, as it was designed by a Chicago architectural firm

distant past can offer valuable lessons to architects who deal in green building. Hundreds of years ago, people did not have the luxury of flipping a switch to heat, cool, or light their homes. An ancient Middle Eastern cooling system inspired what is called a passive downdraft evaporative cooling system being researched in Europe. For centuries, people built wind catchers to direct air over water pots. As the water evaporated, the temperature would drop. Using this system today, an office building can catch wind in special towers and send it into the building. Nozzles spray water into the airflow, and the liquid turns into vapor, which cools the air and improves the air quality.

GREEN METHODS UNPROVEN

Because they are new, many "green" building techniques and materials are today viewed as unproven and unreliable—potentially leading to what architects call "building failure." For example, vegetative roofs are more likely to have problems than traditional roofs because they are constantly wet. Leaking water will damage a structure and possibly lead to mold growth. Also, traditional buildings are tightly sealed to control humidity. Green buildings introduce more outside air, which can cause a higher indoor humidity and mold. As a result, green buildings often come with higher maintenance costs—as well as insurance coverage—in case something goes wrong, or "fails."

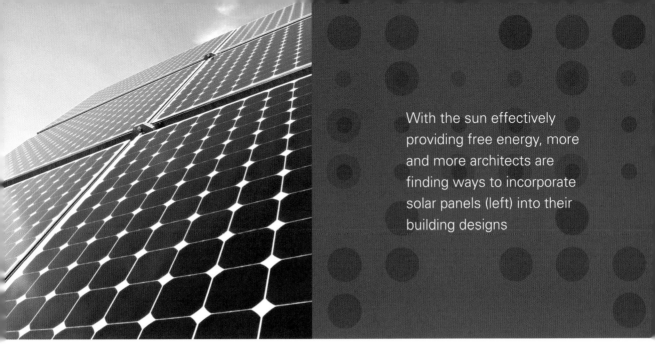

With the sun effectively providing free energy, more and more architects are finding ways to incorporate solar panels (left) into their building designs

To help encourage builders and their clients to plan their projects in a way that is less harmful to the environment, the U.S. Green Building Council has come up with a set of standards. Architects and builders can apply for their projects to be LEED (Leadership in Energy & Environmental Design) certified. Builders in the U.S. and other countries can do a few things—such as simply adding solar panels to their designs—or many to attain one of several levels of LEED certification. For example, the Oregon Health & Science University opened a 16-story Center for Health and Healing in 2006 that was awarded platinum LEED status. While most buildings are tightly sealed to keep nature out, this building allows more natural **ventilation** with a system that draws air through the structure. The heat of the lights and computers helps to circulate the air. Solar shades on the south side of the building generate electricity through solar power, and the building also features a "green" roof that collects rainwater for use in toilets and landscaping.

Architectural blueprints
(right) are the first step
toward the creation of
any significant building—
and the resulting skylines
of cities such as New
York (below)

These building trends pose new challenges to architects. Instead of simply designing the same building in New York as they would in Tokyo, architects must look at each building site and decide on the position and shape of the structure. They must consider the environment; is it usually sunny or cloudy, windy or calm? Designers are able to meet these challenges using computer-aided design programs and other software. In the past, architects sketched their projects on paper, which could be lost or ruined. Computerized designs can be easily stored, saved, and shared with other people working on the project. Using design software, architects can produce both two-dimensional and three-dimensional models, look at their design from different angles, and easily

ELEVATORS LIFT PEOPLE, BUILDINGS

For centuries, people have used lifts, featuring ropes and pulleys, to transport wood and other materials to various levels of a building project. American Elisha Graves Otis did not invent the elevator, but he did design a backup system in 1852 to hold the lift if the rope broke. He also realized that these lifts, fitted with the safety system, could carry people. By 1857, department stores in New York featured the first passenger elevators. The ability to move people and objects up and down quickly and easily allowed architects to design taller buildings. Soon, skyscrapers began popping up on the New York skyline.

experiment with sizes and shapes. If one element of the design is changed, the software will apply the change to the entire structure. Architects also use these programs to anticipate how the building will behave in various weather conditions.

Canadian-born American architect Frank Gehry uses sophisticated design software originally meant for the aeronautics industry. Perhaps that's why his buildings frequently showcase curving metal walls with reflective surfaces. The world-famous architect has been known for "sculpitecture" since his work on the Guggenheim Museum Bilbao in Spain, which opened in 1997. Made with titanium panels that move and reflect different colors in the wind, the Guggenheim Bilbao is a complete break from traditional architectural styles. Gehry's latest project was a 76-story New York highrise, devoted mostly to residential units, which opened in 2011. Called Beekman Tower, and also known as New York by Gehry, the structure features a stainless-steel surface that appears to crease and ripple like fabric. Gehry says that recent developments in computer software have enabled him to create the structures he had always wanted to build but previously could not. The new technology gives his buildings a warm feel as well as a sense of movement, contrasting with the solid coldness of hard edges. "I've been playing with this issue of folds for years," Gehry explains. "They humanize the building."

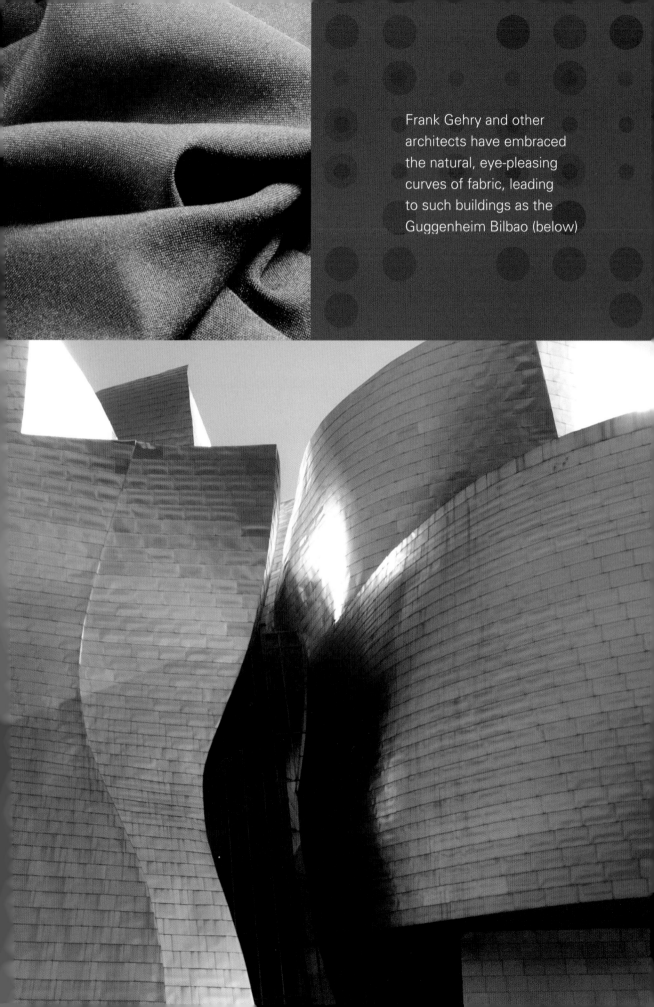

Frank Gehry and other architects have embraced the natural, eye-pleasing curves of fabric, leading to such buildings as the Guggenheim Bilbao (below)

DESIGNS ON THE FUTURE

In the near future, experts predict that the population of the world will increasingly shift from rural to urban areas. In 2007, about 49 percent of people worldwide lived in urban areas. By 2030, researchers expect that about 60 percent of the world's population will reside in cities. Between 2010 and 2050, the amount of developed land on Earth is expected to double. Also, those people in or on the verge of retirement will make up a larger percentage of the world's population. To provide living spaces and clean water to all these people, the trend in design will need to go much farther than simply "sustaining" the environment. Architects will need to find ways to build structures that are actually good for the environment. Keeping the environment and conservation in mind, architects in the future will need to find ways to house people with easy access to health care, jobs, and other businesses. Some already have ideas about how buildings of the future will look and function.

Italian architect David Fisher has designed, but not yet built, what could be the skyscraper of the future. The Dynamic Tower, a residential building planned for Dubai, will differ from other skyscrapers in its ability to rotate and generate its own energy with wind turbines installed between each of its 80 floors. In addition, the pieces of the tower will be prefabricated; each residential unit will arrive at the building site already constructed, complete with electrical wiring and plumbing. The structure is planned to be the first skyscraper to be assembled almost entirely in a factory rather than on location. Fisher said this preconstruction will make the job

The Dynamic Tower, shown here in a sketch, could prove to be a game-changer in the world of architecture with its green design features and ability to rotate

PRESERVATION VERSUS CONSERVATION

New homes have hit the market with more efficient heating and cooling systems, better insulation, and more energy-saving features than ever before. But what about centuries-old mansions and other buildings **preserved** *for their historical importance? While architects and historians alike want to restore these landmarks so they survive for future generations to enjoy, many disagree about adding clean energy systems such as solar panels or wind turbines. In Wisconsin, a preservation office denied an attempt to keep a Frank Lloyd Wright-designed cottage warmer by double-glazing the windows. However, others favor such changes, pointing out that many historic homes have undergone electrical heating and lighting updates throughout the years.*

go more quickly and require fewer workers. He predicts that fewer than 700 laborers and technicians will be able to build the tower in less than 2 years, instead of the more typical 2,000 workers at twice the time.

Each story of the Dynamic Tower will be able to turn at its own speed and direction. As a result, one window will be able to enjoy both sunrise and sunset, and balcony gardens will receive maximum sunlight. With solar panels and wind turbines on each floor, the tower will harness enough energy to power itself as well as other neighboring structures. Fisher's project is ambitious, as he has never before built a skyscraper.

Similar to the Dynamic Tower are "responsive structures," buildings that will be able to alter their shapes depending on the weather. While the Dynamic Tower is supposedly on the horizon within the next few years, responsive structures could take 20 years or more to become reality. In a responsive structure, the building's skeleton will be connected to a robot-like computer system that allows it to react to its environment by bracing itself against high winds or shaking snow from its roof. The inspiration for this type of building comes from nature. John Folan, architect and professor at Carnegie Mellon University in Pittsburgh, Pennsylvania, noted that a building that "truly responds to the environment like a natural organism would be the most successful form of adaptive construction." After all, trees that bend are stronger and lighter than trees that don't. These buildings would be made of light material—rods and wires controlled by air pressure—that can gently swivel in the wind and allow the breeze to blow right through, reducing the stress on the building and allowing architects to build even taller structures that take up less space.

So-called "eco houses," in which vegetation is a part of the structure, face challenges in dealing with water, but they blend beautifully into their environments

Farther into the future are new styles of prefabricated homes, which borrow some ideas from the Dynamic Tower. Although many people currently believe that pre-made homes are of lower quality than those built on location, "prefab" could mean better energy efficiency. Imagine a three-story home consisting of three stacked, prefabricated containers. This design is more compact than a traditional house, saving space in urban locations.

Perhaps future buildings will not only *act* like trees, swaying in the wind, but they will also *look* more like trees. American architect William McDonough envisions future houses designed like trees. The top would absorb sunlight with a **photosynthetic** material woven into the outside of the roof, just as the leaves of trees take in sunlight. This would not only heat the household's water and generate electricity, but the process would also produce oxygen, as plants do. The roof would curve down over the house to provide shade and insulation. An outdoor garden could reside on the roof or creep down the side of the house on a **trellis**. The fruits and vegetables grown there would provide meals as well as shade.

Microsoft and other companies worked with Disneyland in California to build an updated house of the future, called the Innoventions Dream Home, which opened at the theme park in 2008. The design of this house, on display at Disneyland, focuses more on the technology networked into the home than the style of the house itself. The bedroom features a "magic mirror," which

MERGING HOMES WITH NATURE

The son of a teacher and a Baptist minister, Frank Lloyd Wright was one of the most influential architects of the 20th century. Although he built commercial structures, such as New York's Solomon R. Guggenheim Museum, he preferred building for the common man rather than for the wealthy. His home designs were characterized by open floor space and horizontal—rather than vertical—structuring, and they reflected the idea that buildings should blend in with their natural surroundings. For example, instead of designing a house facing a waterfall, Wright designed the house to be positioned above the waterfall. He believed that a house should look as if it had grown out of the landscape.

keeps track of the clothing in the closet and can display how outfits from the closet will look on a person. Similarly, the kitchen is programmed to track how much food—and which kinds—are stored there. Consequently, it can compile a grocery list for the homeowner and display recipe choices based on the foods currently available in the house. The home also offers a new experience in story time, as the entire bedroom adapts to the tale. For example, as a mother reads *Goodnight Moon* to her child, the bedroom turns green to coincide with the phrase, "in the great green room."

Looking farther into the future and at the potential for worldwide catastrophe, Belgian architect Vincent Callebaut has designed a new home for residents in London, New York, Tokyo, and other coastal areas that might lose their cities to rising oceans. The Intergovernmental Panel on Climate Change has suggested that sea levels around the globe could rise as much as three feet (.9 m) by 2100 as a result of global warming and melting polar ice caps. Where would the millions of **displaced** people find shelter? According to Callebaut, they could take refuge in his "Lilypad Cities," each capable of housing 50,000 residents. Taking advantage of a variety of **renewable** energy sources such as solar, thermal, and wind energy, as well as energy from the ocean waves, the lily pads would permanently float in the ocean currents, producing more energy than they use. Each city would be covered by

Oil-rich countries such the UAE (home to the Palm Jumeirah island, opposite, and the Aldar HQ building, left) today lead the way in innovative architecture

suspended gardens and have a lake in the center for collecting and purifying rainwater. Callebaut described his design as a long-term solution. "I think trying to accommodate the millions of people left homeless by environmental changes will prove to be one of the great challenges of the 21st century," he said.

The realm of self-contained cities, however, is not that far away. British architect Norman Foster has already designed an entire city, called Masdar City, near Abu Dhabi in the UAE. The glass-enclosed city will rely solely on solar and wind power for its energy needs and emit no pollution. Residents will be able to live, work, and play in Masdar City, traveling in small cars moved on a network of roads by magnetic **sensor**. The city, capable of accom-modating up to 40,000 residents, could be complete in 3 years or 30, depending on financing and the success of the building process. Foster and other architects have already begun planning enclosed cities in other parts of the world.

CREATIVITY AND COLLABORATION

Some changes in architecture are just over the horizon. Others concepts, such as self-contained, floating cities, seem more far-fetched—the stuff of science-fiction stories. To make any of these futuristic designs a reality, architects and others involved in building will need to use creativity in the face of challenges and work together on ways to design for future generations. "There will be enormous pressure from all directions on stewardship of the environment," said James Cramer, a consultant and former chief executive of the American Institute of Architects in Washington, D.C. "Green construction and innovation is inevitable."

Before architects can set a building project into motion, the person paying for the building must approve of it. The trend toward green, or sustainable, building has come about, in part, because clients have felt an **incentive** to change. Often, it takes a major event or catastrophe to spur changes in the way things are done. During the 1980s, 1990s, and even early 2000s, architects (and the clients hiring them) looked for ways to build larger, more complex and showy buildings. But by 2008, fewer people were buying houses. Others could not keep up with their house payments. Banks, which couldn't get money from people who couldn't pay, needed help from governments. The world economy floundered, and people began to realize they had to live within their means—which in many cases meant buying a smaller house, living in an apartment, or taking in a roommate.

The slump in the world economy that began around 2008 forced many people to live on smaller budgets and left many large buildings with vacant spaces

SALES

RENTALS

IMMEDIATE OCCUPANCY

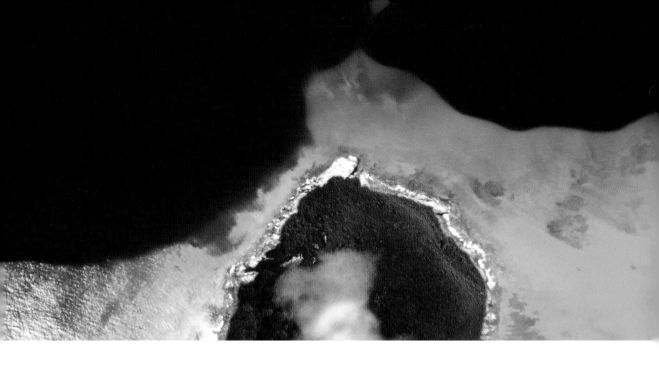

In 2010, the largest oil spill in U.S. history flooded the Gulf of Mexico with more than 200 million gallons (757 million l) of oil, killing sea life and coating miles of beaches with sludge. This crisis emphasized the need for people and businesses to help preserve the environment—to use fewer natural resources and avoid polluting the air and water so that future generations will be able to flourish. These difficult times also bring opportunities for those who will creatively design smaller structures to accommodate what society wants. Around the globe, leaders and planners are forecasting population growth and looking for ways to house more people in less space while providing clean energy. Perhaps other events or disasters will create an even greater urgency for green building.

Education and research will likely fuel more creativity. The Nottingham School of the Built Environment in England runs the Center for Sustainable Energy Technologies, which conducts research and develops and tests new designs for energy efficiency and renewable energy. At the University of California at San Diego, the Structural Systems and Control Laboratory has developed an entirely new branch of mathematics to help create buildings that behave more like a living organism. Perhaps houses could be built more like cars, with complex systems that react to road conditions.

Advances in the tools and materials architects use will give designers more freedom to work new ideas into real structures. Computer technology currently allows architects to create

As architects move into a design age that involves holograms (right), they must increasingly be aware of environmental threats above and beyond oil spills (opposite)

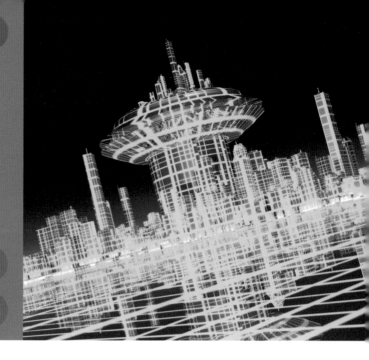

three-dimensional images of their projects, but soon, they will likely be using **holograms** to review their work. Holograms are in the early stages in the building industry, but they were originally created for use in the military. By 2009, maps of cities such as Baghdad, Iraq, sprang off a sheet of thin photographic film under a light in the form of holograms that U.S. military personnel could study to navigate their way through combat zones during the Iraq War. For architecture, holograms could eventually take the place of the models architects build to show clients and investors what the building will look like. A hologram would be much easier and faster to produce than a physical model, and the hologram could also help architects

H. G. WELLS PREDICTS ARCOLOGY

In 1899, H. G. Wells, the English author of classic science-fiction novels such as The Time Machine, *published* When the Sleeper Wakes, *which describes skyscrapers as well as the idea of an enclosed city where residents work, live, and play within one structure. The "sleeper" is a young Englishman who falls into a trancelike sleep that lasts 203 years. He wakes to a futuristic London, where residents travel on moving roads, narrow bridges suspended between tall buildings, and elevators. The entire city is encased in glass. In 1969, Italian-American architect Paolo Soleri described "arcology," the blending of architecture and ecology, and his dream to build a city in a three-dimensional form.*

WORLD'S FAIR STRETCHES IMAGINATIONS

Since the early 1850s, countries have taken turns hosting the World's Fair, a showcase of innovative designs and culture that usually takes place within five years of the previous one. Fairgoers have enjoyed seeing new scientific advances and glimpses of what life might be like in the future. Beginning with the enormous glass and iron Crystal Palace in London at the first fair in 1851, the World's Fair has produced several famous buildings. The Eiffel Tower was built as the entrance arch of the 1889 Expo, held in Paris. In 1962, the fair came to Seattle, Washington, for the unveiling of the Space Needle, which is now a symbol for the city. The 2015 fair was to be hosted by Milan, Italy.

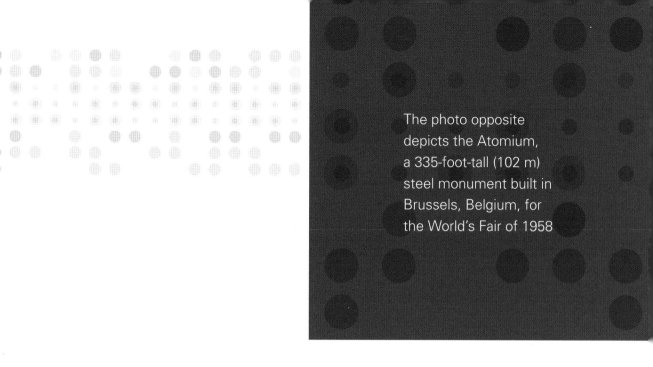

The photo opposite depicts the Atomium, a 335-foot-tall (102 m) steel monument built in Brussels, Belgium, for the World's Fair of 1958

look at their designs to determine whether the building would be feasible in the real world.

As video-game technology has improved, the game characters and their worlds have come to resemble reality. If put to use in architecture, the game world could enable architects to use their creativity in designing a building and allow them to "play test" the structure, evaluating how the size, shape, and materials used would behave in the real world. The clients themselves would be able to virtually tour the building in the game world and decide what they like or dislike about the design.

Just as researchers are updating design tools, scientists are working hard to create new materials to allow creativity in the design of homes, offices, and other buildings. For example, scientists are working with solar panels in an effort to integrate them into building materials so that an observer would not be able to see a panel on the roof of a building.

Another area of research involves bricks, a building material that has been used for thousands of years. As of 2011, American architect Ginger Krieg Dosier was researching methods of making more energy-efficient bricks. Dosier "grows" Lego-sized bricks by combining common bacteria, calcium chloride, urea (a nitrogen-containing substance usually found in urine), and sand. A chemical reaction binds the sand particles together, and the resulting material can be as strong as a traditional brick or even marble. Baking bricks

in a coal-powered kiln—which is the time-tested method—is incredibly destructive to the environment. Not only are trees cut down and burned to make bricks, but the baking process emits roughly 1.3 pounds (.6 kg) of carbon dioxide per brick. Using Dosier's bricks instead could reduce the amount of carbon dioxide released into the environment by 800 million tons (728 million t) each year. But her new brick is still experimental. Before builders could use it, Dosier would need to figure out how to produce it more quickly, since the "biobrick" takes a week to grow, while traditional bricks are made in two days. Also, Dosier needed to find a way to prevent her brick from emitting ammonia, which changes to nitrous oxide, a gas even more harmful to the environment than carbon dioxide.

Along with creativity, architects will need to use collaboration, working together with engineers, planners, and scientists to design for future generations. Now, more than ever, architecture is global, and architects can compete for projects nearly anywhere, as well as work with other architects from around the world. Architects are also working more closely with the people who create new materials and technologies. "One of the crucial issues is to have designers work with the people creating the technology to make it more appealing to put on buildings," said architect Frank Gehry.

Zaha Hadid, an Iraqi-born architect now based in London, also says that new technologies and materials will be pivotal to the future of architecture. These new concepts will promote harmony

Brick and cement
constructions, the MAXXI
museum in Rome, and
the Glasgow Museum
of Transport in Scotland
(left to right) all feature
unconventional angles

with nature, an idea evident in Hadid's designs. One of her latest creations is the London Aquatics Center, built for the 2012 Summer Olympics. The roof, made of curved steel, resembles a stingray and is designed to twist and stretch with the weather. "I don't think that architecture is only about shelter, is only about a very simple enclosure," said Hadid. "It should be able to excite you, to calm you, to make you think."

Ever since the earliest towers and pyramids, people have been designing buildings for safety, as an art form, and as a way to gain fame. Despite the advancements and changes in architecture, the past can educate and help future architects unlock ways of developing useful yet comfortable homes and workplaces. Technology will be the key to creative designs that will align buildings with nature. In 30 years, what will you call "home, sweet home?" Will you have a house that can shake off snow and rain, a home that can help you make your grocery list, or a unit in a floating ocean community? It's possible that you may have these choices—among many others.

GLOSSARY

aeronautics — the design and construction of aircraft

aqueducts — artificial channels made to transport water from one location to another

Bessemer process — a method for making steel by blasting compressed air through melted iron to burn out carbon and impurities

catastrophes — great and often sudden disasters that affect many people

columns — pillars used in building construction; they are typically used for support but may be purely decorative as well

condensation — the process by which water vapor changes to a liquid

displaced — moved out of the usual place

fossil fuels — naturally occurring fuels, such as petroleum, coal, or natural gas, formed by the breakdown of ancient plants and animals; the gases from burning these fuels are believed to contribute to global warming

holograms — images that appear three-dimensional under certain lighting, even though they were printed on a two-dimensional surface

iconic — describing something of such great fame that it comes to stand for something larger, such as a city or culture

incentive — a reward or encouragement that prompts someone to take a certain action

opulent — lavish, or possessing great wealth

photosynthetic — describing the process of taking sunlight and converting it to stored energy

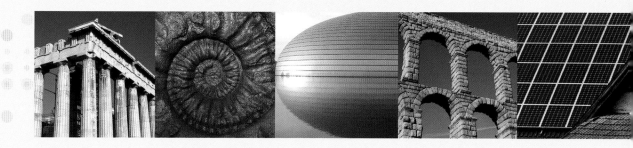

portico — a porch or walkway, usually at the front of a building, that has a roof supported by columns

prefabricated — manufactured in advance, especially in standard sections that can be easily shipped and assembled elsewhere

preserved — protected from injury, change, or danger

remnants — surviving traces of something that no longer exists

renewable — able to be restored

sensor — a device that detects and responds to a signal

suspended — supported up in the air

Teflon — a waxy material that is resistant to acid and is often used on cookware

titanium — a lightweight metal that is very strong and resistant to rusting or staining

trellis — a framework used as a support for growing vines or plants

vaults — rooms or spaces having arched walls and ceilings

ventilation — the act of letting fresh air into a space to replace stale air

SELECTED BIBLIOGRAPHY

Aaltonen, Gaynor. *The History of Architecture*. New York: Metro Books, 2008.

Architect Magazine. "AEC Megatrends: A Vision of the Future." September 9, 2010.

Frangos, Alex. "The Green House of the Future." *Wall Street Journal*, April 27, 2009.

Glancey, Jonathan. "Review of the Decade: Jonathan Glancey on Architecture." *Guardian* (London), December 8, 2009.

———. *The Story of Architecture*. New York: Dorling Kindersley, 2000.

Sandhana, Lakshmi. "Smart Buildings Make Smooth Moves." *Wired*, August 31, 2006.

Wilkinson, Philip. *Building*. New York: Dorling Kindersley, 2000.

WEB SITES

The ArchitectureWeek Great Buildings Collection
http://www.greatbuildings.com/
Find photos and information on 1,000 classic architectural creations from around the globe, along with biographical information on the world's greatest architects.

Dubai Architecture
http://www.dubai-architecture.info/
This site spotlights the architectural marvels of the city of Dubai, home to some of the biggest and most inventive buildings in the world, such as the Burj Al Arab.

INDEX

40 Wall Street 14
Anthemius of Tralles 11
arcology 39
Beekman Tower 26
Bessemer process 14
building materials 6, 8, 9, 11, 13, 14, 16, 19, 20, 26, 41, 42, 43
   cast iron 11, 13, 14
   cement 9, 19
   clay bricks 6, 13, 20, 41, 42
   energy-efficient bricks 41, 42
   ETFE 16, 19
   granite 6
   limestone 8
   marble 9, 41
   steel 14, 20, 26, 43
   titanium 16, 26
Burj Al Arab 19
Burj Khalifa 19–20
Callebaut, Vincent 34–35
Callicrates 8
castles 11
   Tower of London 11
Chrysler Building 14, 19
churches 11
   Hagia Sophia 11
Classical style 13
color changes 4
columns 8–9
computerized designs 25–26, 38–39, 41
   holograms 39, 41
   video-game software 41
Cramer, James 36
Crystal Palace 40
domes 9, 11, 13
Dosier, Ginger Krieg 41, 42
Dynamic Tower 28, 31, 32

Egyptian pyramids 6, 8
   Pyramids of Giza 8
   Step Pyramid of Djoser 6
Eiffel, Alexandre Gustave 13
Eiffel Tower 13, 40
elevators 25
Empire State Building 14, 19
energy conservation 4
Fisher, David 28, 31
Folan, John 31
Foster, Norman 35
Gehry, Frank 26, 42
Great Wall of China 11
green building 20, 22–23, 25, 28, 36, 38
Guggenheim Museum Bilbao 26
Hadid, Zaha 42–43
Hadrian 9
heat reflection 4
heat retention 4
height records 13, 14, 19
Ictinus 8
Imhotep 6
Innoventions Dream Home 32, 34
International style 20
Isidore of Miletus 11
Lilypad Cities 34–35
London Aquatics Center 43
Masdar City 35
McDonough, William 32
National Grand Theater (Beijing) 16
National Stadium (Beijing) 16
Oregon Health & Science University Center for Health and Healing 23
Palladio, Andrea 13
passive downdraft evaporative cooling system 22

pollution reduction 4, 20, 35, 38, 42
prefabrication 11, 28, 31, 32
preservation of historic buildings 30
rainwater collection 4, 23, 35
responsive structures 31, 43
Roman aqueducts 9
roof gardens 32
rotating buildings 31
self-contained cities 35, 36, 39
Severance, H. Craig 14
solar energy 15, 20, 23, 30, 31, 32, 34, 35, 41
   and photosynthetic material 32
Soleri, Paolo 39
Solomon R. Guggenheim Museum 33
Space Needle 40
Teflon 19
temples 6, 8–9, 13
   Pantheon 9, 13
   Parthenon 8–9
   Ziggurat of Ur 6
thermal energy 34
U.S. Green Building Council 23
   LEED certification 23
Van Alen, William 14
Villa Capra 13
Vitruvius 8–9
Wells, H. G. 39
   When the Sleeper Wakes 39
wind energy 14, 20, 28, 30, 31, 34, 35
World's Fairs 40
Wright, Frank Lloyd 30, 33

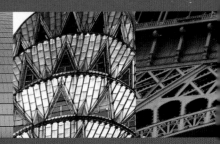

Published by Creative Education
P.O. Box 227, Mankato, Minnesota 56002
Creative Education is an imprint of The Creative Company
www.thecreativecompany.us

Design and production by The Design Lab
Art direction by Rita Marshall
Printed in the United States of America

Photographs by Alamy (Andy Buchanan, Michelle Chaplow), Corbis (Keats/Retna
Ltd., Charles & Josette Lenars), Dreamstime (Ahdrum, Alexmax, Athenar, Banol2007,
Keith Barlow, Brighton, Davinci, Enrico De Vita, Sergey Denisov, Serban Enache, Luis
Estallo, Sergio Fabbri, Vasiliy Ganzha, Victor Habbick, Hurry, Italianestro, Jarnogz,
Jjspring, Kjersti Joergensen, Kajanek, Anett Kneifel, Vladimir Korostyshevsky, Daniel
Korzeniewski, Melinda Nagy, Stephen Orsillo, Lambert Parren, Carlos Sanchez Pereyra,
Photoniles, Pictura, Podaril, Shariff Che' Lah, Darryl Sleath, Sofiaworld, Dmitriy
Suzyumov), Shutterstock (Frank Gaertner, haider, hainaultphoto)

Library of Congress Cataloging-in-Publication Data

Dittmer, Lori.
The future of architecture / by Lori Dittmer.
p. cm. — (What's next?)
Includes bibliographical references and index.
Summary: A look at potential future developments in architecture, including self-
contained cities, as well as computerized blueprints and other technologies that are
currently considered state-of-the-art.
ISBN 978-1-60818-220-6
1. Architecture—Forecasting. 2. Architecture—Technological innovations.
3. Architectural design. I. Title.

NA2540.D58 2012
720.1'12—dc23   2011040503

First edition

9 8 7 6 5 4 3 2 1

Cover: The Welsh National Assembly building, Cardiff, Wales
Page 1: Loket Castle, Czech Republic
Page 2: The Solomon R. Guggenheim Museum, New York, New York